Rooms with Chairs

ReMind™

Mara M. Zimmerman

Balboa Press books may be ordered through booksellers or by contacting:

Balboa Press
A Division of Hay House
1663 Liberty Drive
Bloomington, IN 47403
www.balboapress.com
844-682-1282

Interior Image Credit: Mara M. Zimmerman

ISBN: 979-8-7652-4275-9 (sc)
ISBN: 979-8-7652-4276-6 (e)

Library of Congress Control Number: 2023910049

Print information available on the last page.

Balboa Press rev. date: 06/13/2023

BALBOA.PRESS
A DIVISION OF HAY HOUSE

A guided chair meditation

Welcome.

Good posture.

Balanced breathing.

Be mindful.

Move both sides

of the body for balance.

Easy does it.

Enjoy.

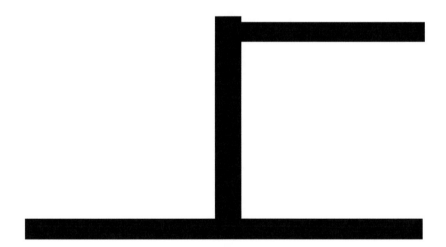

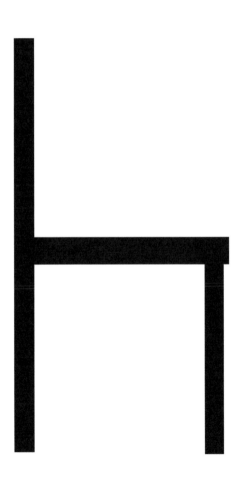

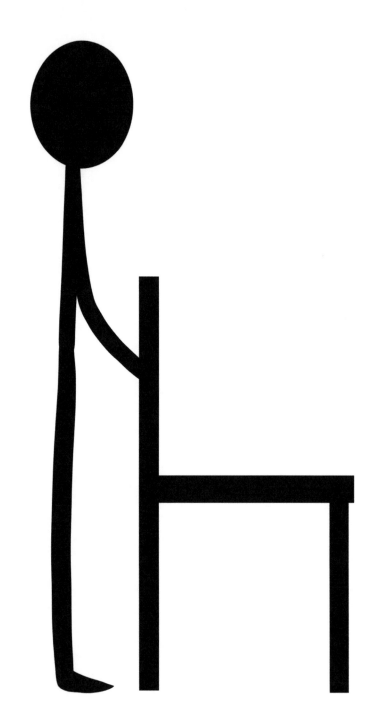

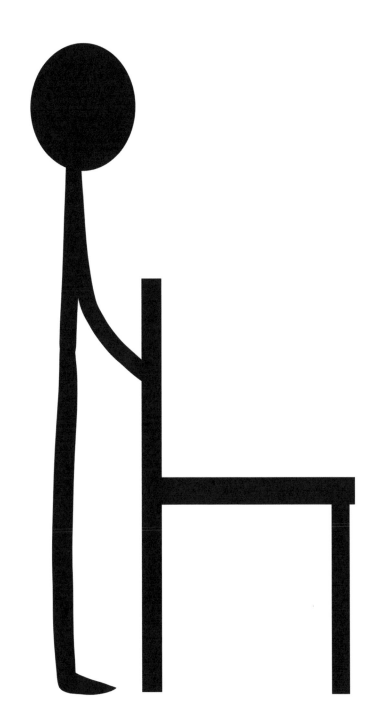

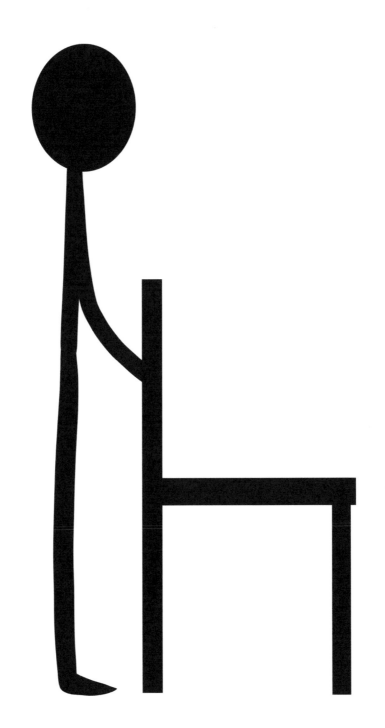

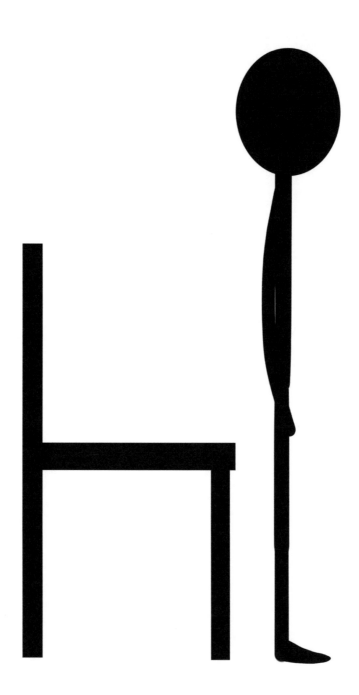

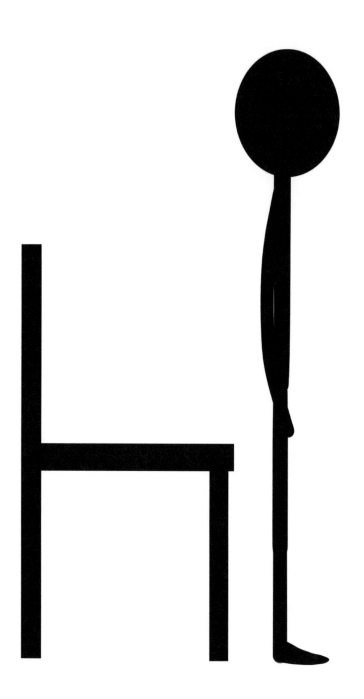

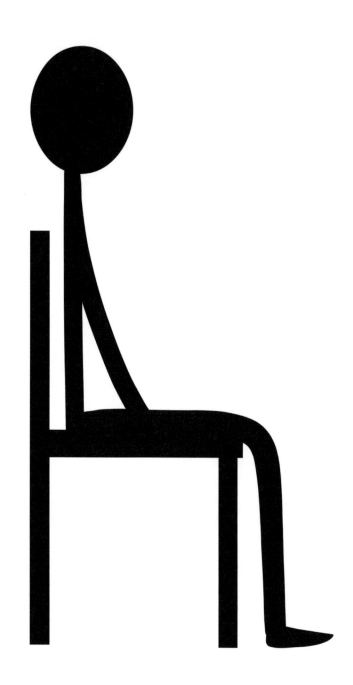

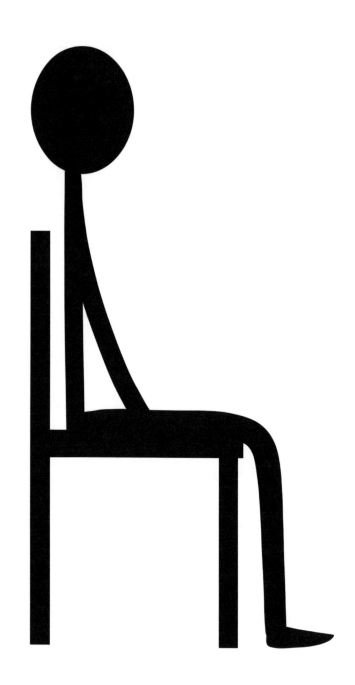

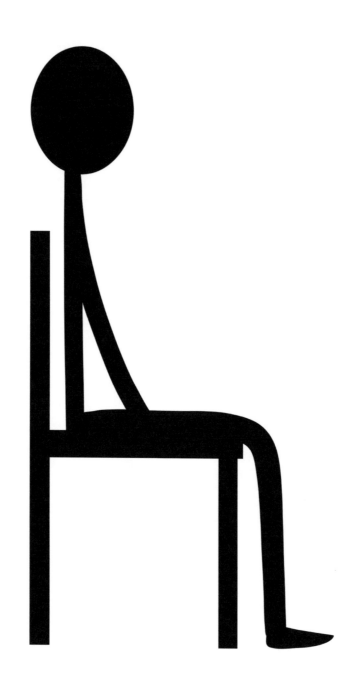

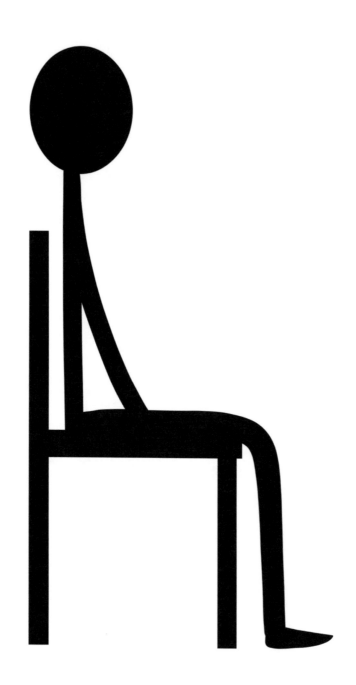

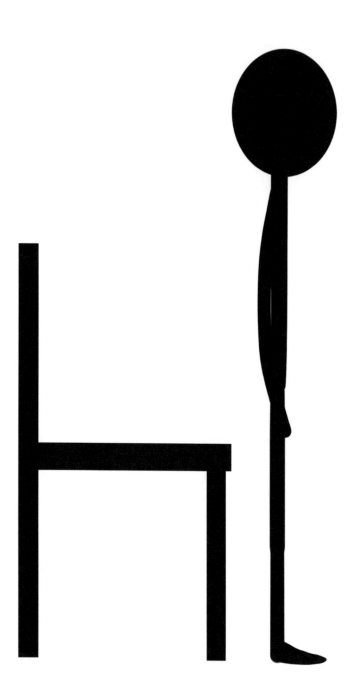

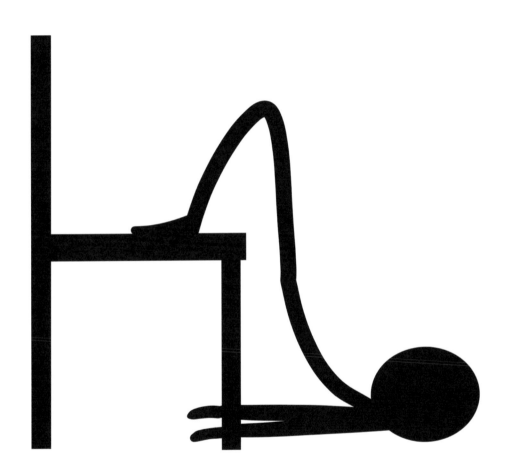

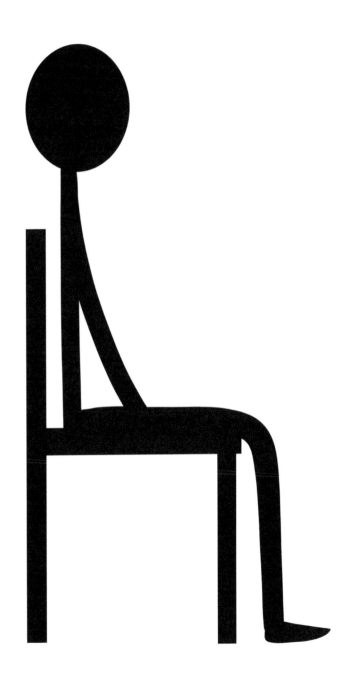

29

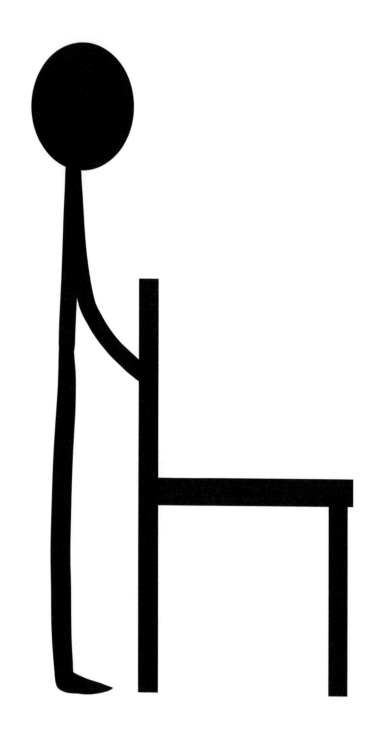

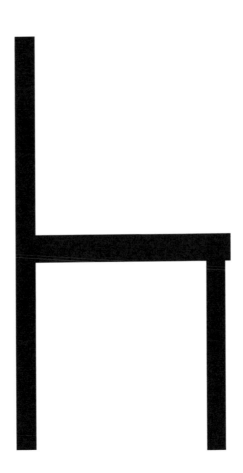

About the Author

Mara M. Zimmerman has been teaching Yoga, Meditation and Mindfulness to all ages in educational and therapeutic spaces throughout her career. She is the creator of ReMind, a program for optimal well-being, for all ages.

More books in this series:

ReMind: Building Rocks of Mindfulness with Stepping Stones

ReMind: Building Rocks of Mindfulness with Jewish Stepping Stones

ReMind: Yoga with Alef

and

How to Meditate and Why

For more information, please visit
maramzimmerman.com

Printed in the United States
by Baker & Taylor Publisher Services